INTERVIEW SKILLS

Essential guidelines to successful interviews

Dr. Aubrey Tsebe

Bethel Institute of Leadership Publishers

Bethel Institute of Leadership (BIL)

Brooklyn Bridge Office Park

570 Ferhrsen

Building 2, 3rd Floor

Pretoria, 0018

info@biol.co.za

publishers@biol.co.za

ISBN: 978-0-620-96477-7

Bethel Institute of Leadership Publishers (BILPub) is a division of Bethel Institute of Leadership (BIL). BILPub name and logo are trademarks of BIL.

Let's keep in touch:

Please follow us on the follow us on our social media handles:

	bilpublishers
	BIL TV ***Dr Aubrey***
	BIL-TV

The contents of this book are offered as part of an Interview Skills Course at Udemy. Please go to the Udemy website to access the course should you be interested in the entire presentation about this course.

Use this link to access the course and promotions:
https://www.udemy.com/course/my-interviewing-skills-course/?referralCode=41F6D5436BABE33CB449

DEDICATION:

I dedicate this book to all my clients, who have opened my eyes to the reality of their failed job seeking endeavours. I hope that this book will serve as motivation that it is still possible to try again and secure your job. This book is also dedicated to all my students worldwide who have benefited from our online course. Thank you for being part of our online family; your support and feedback have helped me help others.

CONTENTS

INTRODUCTION

Everyone needs to have some level of interview skills. It does not matter whether you are a student, an employee, a businessman or a boss; you will interview skills at various points of your personal and professional life. Interview skills allow you to successfully access key information as an interviewer and to produce key information as an interviewee. If you think about it many of our interactions are interviews, let me prove it to you. Dating that great girl or man and want to assess if he/she is "the one" you engage in a series of questions and interactions that help you access and assess whether he/she is the "suitable candidate". Looking for a math's tutor? You conduct an interview, not sure what to order on the menu? You "interview" the waiter on the best options. I could go on, but I am sure you are catching my drift, we are constantly interviewing and being interviewed beyond the context of job seeking. Some interviews are more formal than others, require more skills but essentially, they are interviews. I think we can now agree that there is no person who can claim to have never been in some form of an interview. It is, therefore, essential that you are equipped with these skills for such reasons. Interview skills are not only a job seeking skill but are really a life skill. I have developed a course titled, Interviewing Skills, Conducting a successful job interview. The course is hosted on Udemy for developmental purposes. I have included a snippet of the course in my YouTube Channel as well. I recommend that you also check it out to access the discount coupon for the course or send us an email and we will send you a discount code.

As a psychologist, I have come across many clients who struggle to secure a job, even before the Coronavirus- 2019 (COVID-19), implying that the pandemic might not be the main reason you are not working. Some people progress to the interview stage in their job seeking journey but struggle to successfully progress form interview to the employment phase. I decided to write this book so that you can start to have successful job interviews, who knows, if you apply the principles in this book, you might find yourself interviewing your potential employer to assess the suitability of the job for your specific needs. It's possible!!!

> *A person can prepare a lot for a job interview only to lose a job after a few months due to a lack of post-interview skills.*

I have compiled this book to achieve two purposes. Firstly, to provide you with the essential skills necessary for you to have a successful interview. It serves as a supplemental resource for the afore-mentioned course that you can refer to every time you prepare for an interview or get a job opportunity. In essence, it can also serve as a checklist that you can always rely on to ensure that you are ready for your new work. Secondly, the book aims to provide post-interview tips. People often prepare a lot for a job only to lose it after a few months due to a lack of post-interview skills. I will, therefore, also share some insight about what you can do post the interview to help you secure your job and succeed during your job probation.

<u>Personal Notes</u>

Interview Skills

Reflection Exercise #1

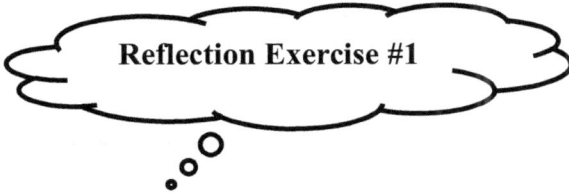

Please take some time to reflect on your past interview experiences. Then, ask yourself the following questions:

• *What kind of interviews were they? (Formal or informal)*

• *Who was interviewing you? (a Friend, or a potential employer)*

• *How was the experience of each interview? Describe your feelings before and after the interview, your thoughts during the interview and after the interview.*

• *In hindsight, what do you think about the above interviews? Are your feelings/thoughts still the same?*

Reflection Notes

Interview Skills

Interview Skills

Interview Reflection

I hope that you found the above exercise fruitful. The lesson is that you have been in some form of an interview at one stage of your life. What is concerning you about the interview is not the interview per se, rather the formality of the interview. That is because you have associated the difficulty of an interview with its formality. You have concluded that the more formal the interview, the difficult it will become. However, interviews are not made difficult by their level of formality; rather, by your lack of readiness. Therefore, you must look at interviews from a different perspective, that the more prepared you are for an interview, the less difficult an interview experience will be for you.

Personal Notes

Interview Skills

Interview Skills

| |
| |
| |
| |
| |
| |
| |
| |
| |
| |
| |
| |
| |
| |
| |
| |
| |

INTERVIEW PREPARATION

We have established in the previous chapter that the essential aspect of an interview is preparation. Preparation is crucial for any successful interview. When I speak about preparing, you might feel that you do not have much information to help you prepare as you do not know what to expect. That is the view that most people have about the interview; they take them as if they will write an exam without a scope of what to expect. However, any interviewer can tell you that is not true. There is a lot of information you have about the job before you come for an interview, and that information can be obtained on the job advertisement. The advert is prepared and publicized because it is a brief about the vacant post to help the potential applicants determine their suitability for the job. Therefore, a good job advert should provide enough information to help you prepare for the post.

I do admit that I have also seen some poorly written job adverts.

Not to mention that I have also been part of an interview panel with bad job adverts, to the extent that tension arises during the shortlisting process as the advert is not clear.

> The advert is the main brief about the vacant post to help the potential applicants determine their suitability for the job and prepare for the interview.

Therefore, it is important to note that there are bad adverts, but that is not your problem as the candidate, rather, that of the panel or the employer, and given an opportunity and if necessary, you can bring it to the attention of the panel.

Reflection Exercise #2

Please take some time to reflect on the job adverts that you have come across. Then, ask yourself the following questions:

- Did you apply for the posts or not?

- Did your above decision have anything to do with the advert?

- What was bad or good about the job advert? (Elaborate further on this)

Reflection Notes

JOB ADVERT

A good job advert will have the following
information:

- Job title/Advertised Position
- Post level or grade
- Type of the post: Permanent/Temporary or
  Contract, etc.
- Name of the hiring organization (Where
  applicable, a division or department might be
  indicated as well)
- Location: A place where the organization is
  located
- *Introduction:* Commonly, a vision statement
  about the organization and the reason why
  the post is needed. The introduction is often
  not titled.
- *Responsibilities*: Main responsibilities to be
  expected of you should you be appointed.
- *Minimum requirements:* The needed
  requirements to be shortlisted. In principle, if

you do not meet the minimum requirements, you will not even be invited for the interview.

- *Added advantage*: Certain attributes or qualifications which you have will add an advantage to your application. The added advantages can only be considered if you meet the minimum requirements.

- *Required competencies*. Competencies that will be required to fulfil the job responsibilities.

- *Remuneration or total packages*: An estimate of how much you might earn per annum or a total package that includes other benefits for the job. Where such information is not provided, numbers of the Human resource personnel should be provided for one to call and inquire about the financial benefits.

- *Contact person for the post*: The contact person can be the human resource personnel or any person with relevant information about the position.

- *Conclusion:* As on the vision statement, the conclusion is also not titled; it refers to the policy or position statement about the advertised position.

Personal Notes

Interview Skills

INTERVIEW PREPARATION: THE CANDIDATE

The following principles are important for the candidate to prepare for an interview:

1. Understand the job or Position

It is your responsibility as the candidate to ensure that you fully understand the job you are applying for. As indicated in the previous section, check the advert thoroughly, for the title of the post, the level and type of appointment. If you are already employed permanently, the type of an appointment for the advertised position can be the determining factor. For example, it might not be a good idea to leave a permanent job for a temporary one, regardless of how lucrative that move might look. However, it is important to note that such a decision might be justifiable when it is strategic decision to exit the permanent work status. Some of us who have been in permanent employment have used the same strategy to get out of the fulltime work and focus on business. The transition must be done gradually to avoid incurring financial loss due to lack of proper planning.

Personal Notes

About the position that you are planning to apply for.

Interview Skills

2. Understand the organization

It is essential that you research the organization you are applying for a job at before trying to join it, especially if you do not know the organization at all. From a legal perspective, many bogus firms use job adverts to lure unsuspecting and vulnerable people. You only realize that you have been trapped when you arrive at the venue and are already captured! Therefore, thorough research on the organization can help you avoid any potential unpleasant ordeal. Although we live in the day of the internet and information should be readily available at the tip of your fingers, it is imperative to do a thorough search to ensure your safety.

Understanding the organization that you plan on joining is also essential to calculate your move. I have seen people leave good jobs only to return after finding out that the place they thought was the "greener pasture" was worse than their current work. To ensure that your move is well calculated, thoroughly research your potential employer, understand their background, current and past issues, reputation and so forth. Check if their vision aligns with yours and whether your possible position will help you reach the heights you aim for in life. Although not all aspects of the organization might be of interest to you, there must at least be some common grounds that justify your move. You must have also assessed the element of fulfilment that you will get by joining the new organization.

Personal Notes

About the Organization that you are planning to apply to.

Interview Skills

3. Demonstrate Competency in the Key Performance Areas (KPAs)

Essentially, the key performance indicators are the main reason they want to employ you. Should you be appointed, the same key performance indicators will serve as your job expectations. They will help you measure your success and monitor your progress. Therefore, when you see an advert, ensure that you thoroughly read the critical performance indicators to know what is expected of you. When answering your interview questions, hinge or refer to these indicators as that is what they will be looking for, regardless of whether they ask you about them or not. It will help if you find ways to strategically slot them in your responses without explicitly mentioning that they are on the advert.

Personal Notes

About the Competencies that you possess

4. Aim for a Lasting Impression

Interviews are about creating an impression. It is absurd to think that twenty (20) minutes to an hour of an interview is sufficient for the panel to know you well enough to decide on your future career move. Errors, misjudgment, and bias are likely to occur, and that can be to your advantage or disadvantage. Therefore, the onus remains with you to make an impression on the panel during the interview, let them feel that they cannot do without you and that you are the best candidate for the job. It is a performance of some sort, and unfortunately, that performance can either earn you a lucrative career or suggest that you are not the 'right fit' for the organization. Therefore, do not play with the opportunity given to you regarding the interview. If you were good enough to be called for an interview, you are also good enough to be appointed. It is up to you to grab your job with both hands.

Personal Notes

About ideas on how you can make impression at an interview.

Interview Skills

Interview Skills

| |
| |
| |
| |
| |
| |
| |
| |
| |
| |
| |
| |
| |
| |
| |
| |
| |

SELF-AWARENESS: WHO AM I?

Many often leave the concept of self-awareness until they enter the interview room, and they are asked, "tell us about yourself?" Only when people start to grapple with this question that they realize that they are not well acquainted with themselves! We often find ourselves in this embarrassing situation because we assume we know ourselves. Although we do, in a general sense, there are some granular details about ourselves that rely on careful observation and constant reflection to understand ourselves fully. Such information about ourselves allows us to respond to the question of who you are appropriately.

> Only when people start to grapple with the "who am I" question that they realize that they are not well acquainted with themselves!

Before I guide you on answering the "Who am I" question, I want you to take some time and reflect on your past experiences with the question.

Reflection Exercise #3

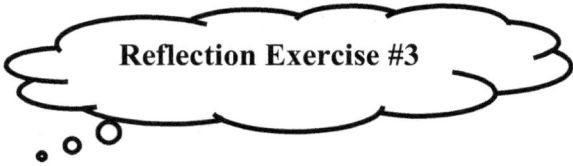

Please take some time to reflect on the interview experiences you attended, where you had to answer the "who am I" question. Reflect on the following questions:

- How was the question phrased?

- What was your response to the question? (Elaborate further on this)

- Were you satisfied with how you responded to the question?

- Did you get a sense that the panel was satisfied with your response?

Reflection Notes

Interview Skills

Self-Knowledge

We often know a lot about our work, gadgets, pets, and many other things around us, but we ignore self-knowledge. Self-knowledge refers to the insight about the core of who you really are. It covers your personality, character, tendencies or inclination and habits. Although many books have been written in psychology and about one's purpose, majority of people are yet to understand the value of understanding oneself. Self-knowledge does not only help you to answer the "who am I" question, it also provides you with the essential tools to help you relate with others better. It is true that when you understand something, you use it appropriately. Therefore, when you understand yourself well, you can take care of yourself in such a way that helps you to relate with others better.

During the *Interview Skill Course*, I shared about three principles that can help you understand yourself. I share about these principles below with some elaboration on them:

Self-analysis

To gain an understanding of yourself, you must often engage in the process of self-analysis. Self-analysis allows you to be your own investigator; you constantly observe yourself, how you behave in different contexts, how you act when you are angry or happy, sad and when you want to achieve a particular goal. Gathering information about yourself will assist you in accurately understanding yourself.

<u>Personal Notes</u>

Write some notes based on how you self-analysed yourself.

Interview Skills

Description by others

One of the exercises you need to do for yourself is to find out how others describe you. In psychology, there is a theory that postulates that there is no slip of the tongue. According to the theory, what one refers to as a slip of the tongue reflects their underlying thoughts. We can often count on our closest friends and family members to better understand ourselves. A true friend will hardly lie to you; rather, they will tell you the truth about who you are. You do not even have to ask them to share how they view you; rather, being attentive to how they describe you to others might be enough. Even listening to them when they share what they have told others about you is enough to give you an insight into how they describe you. Such information from an honest friend will help you understand yourself.

The way others describe it can also help you to be aware of your blind spots. We often assume that we act in a certain way and that people view us the way we want them to see us, but that is not always the case.

For example, I had seen many people who came out of an interview believing that they had mesmerized the panel, only to find out when they did not get the job that they were the only ones who were mesmerized. Therefore, the description of others can also serve as a mirror that can help you reflect on how you present yourself and how others perceive that.

Personal Notes

About how you have discovered others describe you and your thoughts about their description of you.

| |
| |
| |
| |
| |
| |
| |
| |
| |

Interview Skills

Introspection

Related to the principle that I described above is the concept of introspection. When you get feedback from others and don't like what you have, the best thing to do is to engage in introspection. Introspection is when you look inside to understand your inner processes, such as your thoughts and emotions. It helps you understand why you do the things you do, why you say what you say and why you act the way you do. Introspection should lead you to reflect on your behaviour to improve it for the better. Lack of introspection can lead to you sending the wrong message that you do not intend on sending when relating with people. There are people that when you look at them, you wonder if they don't have people close to them who can tell them the truth about themselves. Often such happens because people never take time to introspect. Therefore, you must take time to introspect to gain a more profound and richer understanding of yourself.

Personal Notes

Write some notes based on the introspection about your recent behaviour that you did not like.

Interview Skills

Interview Skills

HOW TO ASNWER THE "WHO AM I" QUESTION?

To appropriately answer the "who am I" question, you first need to understand yourself as described in the previous section. Knowledge about yourself will help you correctly answer the "who am I" question so that it satisfies the panel's expectations. If I take you back to the first section on how to prepare for an interview, I said that your main goal is to convince the panel that you are the best candidate for the position. It all starts with appropriately answering the "who am I" question to convince the panel.

> Knowledge about yourself will help you correctly answer the "who am I" question so that it satisfies the panel's expectations.

The question must be answered within the context of the job. The temptation that many people have, which is also a mistake, is to give elaborate explanations about themselves without any reference to the position they have applied for, which brought them to the interview. To speak about yourself outside the work context is an error that must be avoided as the panel is only interested in your life as it relates to the work. You must understand that a job interview is not a social gathering where you speak about yourself to get to know each other and it ends there; rather, there is a goal which is to be appointed for the advertised post. The panel is interested in learning how your self-description fits into the description of the person they want to appoint. In other words, what they are asking of you is, "who are you in relation to the advertised post?

> The panel is interested in learning how your self-description fits into the description of a person they want to appoint.

For the sake of relevance, when you describe yourself, keep on relating your qualities or competencies with those described in the job advert. Help them connect the dots about the person you are and the job advert.

By so doing, you are making their work easier and building towards confirming that you are the best candidate for them. In essence, by the time you finish your interview, you should have shown them that you are the person they have described in the job advert.

You must understand that a job interview is not a social gathering where you speak about yourself to get to know each other and it ends there; rather, there is a goal which is to be appointed for the advertised post.

Furthermore, you must approach this question chronologically to help the panel understand why you decided to apply for the post. Therefore, you must have a clear storyline. The embarrassing thing that most people do is to answer a question by asking a question. For example, in answering the question, *"could you briefly tell us about yourself and why you applied for this position?"* A person might respond by asking, "there is a lot I can say about myself; perhaps tell me where you want me to start?" As consultative as that might sound, it is not a good question because the question asked by the panel cannot be made easier than it is already. You must know where to start, as your career path has brought you to the interview. Hence, the last part of the sentence often is, *"and why you applied for this position?".* As you describe yourself, this implies that you need to take the panel on a journey that will help them understand why you have applied for the current position. Preparation for the interview must include a plan about how to answer this question.

> You must know where to start in answering the question about yourself, as your career path has brought you to the interview.

I often say the "who am I" question is the only question that you can be guaranteed that it is likely to be asked in the interview, as such you really have no excuse when it comes to answering it. If there is any question that you must do well on in an interview, it is the question about yourself.

In conclusion, when this question is answered appropriately, it serves as the context for all the follow-up interview questions. Based on the broadness of this question, it covers various aspects of your life, which will ultimately be referred to in some follow-up questions. Therefore, when you have answered the question well, all you must do is refer to the first response.

The "who am I" question is the only question that you can be guaranteed that it is likely to be asked in the interview, and therefore, you have no excuse when it comes to answering it.

To fully prepare for this question, you need to understand your career path and past career decisions well. The information mentioned above will help you build a case for your application and assist the panel in understanding why you are the best candidate for the job. Of course, it would help if you excelled in responding to the question about yourself, but you can only do that when you thoroughly prepare for it. Therefore, make sure you follow all the principles I shared about self-knowledge and job advert to help you prepare for this question.

Personal Notes

Interview Skills

Interview Skills

PERSONALITY AND THE INTERVIEW

In this last section, I shift the focus to the most critical aspect of human behaviour, which is your personality. I am referring to personality because that is what you bring to the interview room. An example of personality can best be portrayed by a character acting on any television drama or movie. What keeps us glued to the screen is the personalities that are being presented to us. Unfortunately, what we often see is not real, as far as the characters are concerned.

> What keeps us glued to the television screen is the personalities that are being presented to us.

The actors must get into the role of their characters to portray a particular personality which we then watch as characters of the drama. However, the reality is that all the characters that we fall in love with are fictional. The only real thing is the person acting the character. The world of the entertainment industry has revealed the power of portrayed personalities.

> In order words, we no longer relate with the real person, rather, the personality presented to us.

What interest us the most about these characters is how they are portrayed to reflect the day-to-day issues of real people. In order words, we no longer relate with the real person, rather, the personality that is presented to us.

> We all can portray the personality that we want to present at any instance in our lives we put our mind to it.

We all can portray the personality that we want to present at any instance in our lives we put our mind to it. Talk about job hacking! That is why a panel can appoint a person for a job only to realize later that they appointed the wrong person. Therefore, when you grasp this principle, you will excel in any interview you attend.

What is Personality

Personality is the combination of your character and temperament. Your character is an arrangement of your habits, while temperament is the arrangement of your inclinations. Therefore, when we speak about personality, habits and inclinations play a role in the environment in which personality is demonstrated. Personality is what you portray or act out in any setting. For example, when you go to a funeral, you don't act the same way you do at a wedding or party. Any environment provides a platform or context which guides the appropriate personality that is expected. The same is true with an interview.

> Personality is what you portray or act out in any setting.

When you go for an interview, there are expectations about the person who must get the job. The job advert gives some overarching description of this person. Therefore, it is part of your preparation to ensure that you are fully prepared to act out this person. Your duty is to portray the personality of the person they want. You only have few minutes to make an impression, and you can only do that when you know what the panel expects, so that you can give them what they want, so that they can give you what you want, which is the post

You only have few minutes to make an impression, and you can only do that when you know what the panel expects, so that you can give them what they want, so that they can give you what you want, which is the post

Many people may provide to the panel what they expect, and you end up not being selected; that is still fine as you unlikely to be chosen for all the interviews you attend. As long as you do not leave the interview feeling that you did not do as well as you would have liked, convincing the panel that you are the right person for the job. Your personality is a tool in your hands that you can use to succeed in an interview

Personal Notes

Interview Skills

Interview Skills

Interview Skills

Interview Skills

Interview Skills

Interview Skills

Interview Skills

Interview Skills

Interview Skills

Interview Skills

Interview Skills

Interview Skills

Interview Skills

Interview Skills

Interview Skills

Interview Skills

OTHER BOOKS BY THE AUTHOR

- ✓ Acts of the Holy Spirit: Lessons from the book of Acts
- ✓ Giving: Lessons from the Macedonians
- ✓ The Seasons of God: The key to effective and successful life
- ✓ The Basic Principles of Courtship and Marriage
- ✓ You Are gods: The power of divine election
- ✓ The Keys of The Kingdom Series
- ✓ Faith, Hope & Love: The key to a victorious life
- ✓ Humility: The key to the supernatural
- ✓ Overcoming An offence: The key to a peaceful life
- ✓ Submitting to Authority: key to divine destiny